Time Came Upon Me
& Other Poems

by
MARK NWAGWU

BookBuilders ▪ Editions Africa

Published in Nigeria by
BookBuilders • Editions Africa
2 Awosika Avenue, Bodija, Ibadan
email: bookbuildersafrica@yahoo.com
mobile: 0805 662 9266; 0809 920 9106

In Memory of

My Dear Wife

Helen Onyemazuwa Nwagwu
22 March, 1943 – 30 March, 2018

CONTENTS

1

a day

a day a minute a second
seconds of wit come
as the second laughter
dins minutely into day

2

you must be in the gift

you have to be in the gift you offer
present all you are that's what it's for
representing you in virtue and goodness
for what you are is more than the gift
a thing soon forgotten of little substance
of little meaning
you are jollof rice

3
heavenly taper

how could I have done this to hunt me into
    tomorrows everlasting
every night that drowns dirt, resurrects in sunlight
full blast, evil in ascendance, its whip thrashing the
    limbs
bloodied legs can't walk, swollen eyes can't cry

what invites the past in hot pursuit, never
    exhausted
fast breathing into the morning coffee, the flavour dry
    and drab
all that's good is gone, boils grow in firm skin, sores
    sully the lips
I rise, my eyes on fire burn love's petals

this must end, yesterdays are dead, their rainbows
    have no skies
can't unfurl, their colours insipid fall off
    unaddressed
can't be sewn together

all the good and beauty that could be created
was present in you sparkling, resplendent, they
    speak to my soul
blaze a trail, a heavenly taper lighting the path to
    eternal glow

4
behind you

happy walking behind you
loving your every step
happiest

when you've received communion

all of heaven walks with you

5
epiphany

you wanted someone
who would not only love you
but be enamored of you
so he would never leave you
and if he did - which to you
would be stupid -
he would swiftly fly
back to you
so enthralling
so potent
your presence

6
Smirnoff cold

unknowns creep up, undying, my resolve in sweat
how do I proceed what do I pay attention to
my faith comes to the rescue
tells me what to do, guides me which way to take
am I still who I believe I am, am I still the best I can
    be
I watch I wonder I wait
I must move forward confidence my pal. This is the
    time
I define myself by this final move and I'd be fine

is Helen the one we shall be singing to
and dancing with...
as she drinks her smirnoff cold . . . ?
my soul tumultuous trembles in song

7
sounds

sound absorbs suspicious sounds
heart's delight muffled by pained follies
spider's thoughts escape the web
and words fill the drum to dull the beat

8

bear me up

Mark Nwagwu saw an emerald fire burning in Helen's
    eyes
fifty years ago......
(was) it a heavenly taper lighting the path to higher
    realms....?

               .... Ben Obumselu

a mystery revealed in death
am I able to reach the depths of your soul
am I able to soar to heights beckoning on me
am I able to free myself, give totally of self that I may
    fly

you ask me to meet you in your skies, hold firmly to
    me
raise a wind to bear me to whirling ecstasies

how does this woman live in dazzling detail, I ask
you whisper, I'll live in you on flights to the highest
    realms

9
emerald fire

if the fire burned
undimmed
while you lived
your eyes now burn
indefinitely lit
in heaven's fanning air

10
rendezvous eyes

I search for you and rest my soul
on your rendezvous eyes
the joy the splendour the magnificence
multiplied manifold to Himalayan heights

It's a new alleluia! an inexhaustible dream
I dance on the brilliance of your soul
the brilliance of your mind
the brilliance of your fingers

11
verbs sing your colours

pains paint the years, print their persona
green speaks a language fairies can write
their wings flap right and left, find new nouns
red lights the face pronounces pronouns
drums speak, verbs violet paint brows indigo
oratorical lips dotted yellow describe their adjectives
adverbs move slowly engage orange for singing blues

happy birthday Helen the rainbows herald

12
where will I find you

when you come
you will find me
in heaven beatific

they covered my eyes
they covered my face
mystery's revealed

13
pride pierced

the marvels for all their worth
seek places to show their might
far out in space not known to humans
the mind bewildered seeks solace
bitten, bitter, can't cross the bridge
unknown to eyes in loveless adventure

walk around, the market beckons
its goods sparkle invite purchase
not with gold or anything earthly
virtues respond bring in their wealth
float and fly against the wind
pressure needed not of force
finds flowers in the awkward wind
doom ensnared depression disappears

prudence steps out in a shroud
heroes in the field wave and dance
she's of their ilk, simple
serene meek lowly sublime
her touch a spring of justice
washes away all earthly strife
for that priceless faith, fortitude
glazed on her brow

where's my pride, I slide and turn in frenzy
my worldly coat shouts my opulence
shoes of gold from mines of marrow
leather alive speak in flowing bones

I fall can't find the floor or the ground
the mines too deep can't be reached
suspended, floating, my pride is pierced
temperance returns, kisses my brow, draws me out

14
come to me

come to me that we may swirl in a cup and be drunk
by all who pass our way and wish to slake their thirst
they don't know us nor what they are drinking
all that matters is they can go on their way satisfied
will they ask questions as to the nature of the drink
what wine is this the cheeks chime like morning
    birds
the sun rises, its first rays the vines engage, samba
    the dance
brightness burns the night's dross, all is flowers
we are nature's masterpiece grapes our childhood

15

our tomorrows

where once our hearts on thin air were hung
on hills unknown, vines of grace multitudinous
fructify our transgressing pursuits

where once we grieved filled with anguish
of human struggles, our minds are tuned
to angels, earth and skies sing to children

where once our bodies were seduced by passions
thought to be apostles of joy, our frame is
silken, burnished with aromas of the saints

love of the Niger, our spirit looks far to the Nile
west and east wed, mythical skies their home
pyramids exultant, Eros majestic floods nuptial
    deltas

16
spread your wings

spread your wings full span
the edges touching the ends of east and west
brimful breeze bears you up north to the stars
they've been waiting for you, running around
in circles, seeking your centre
majestic you soar above pristine necks
brightness transcendent they spin in your soul

17
the joy you give me

can't capture the joy you give me
your treasures written in your eyes
you don't see them don't know them
I smile I'm consumed
in the priceless pearls of your eyes

18
to look at you

to look at you, new definitions surprise
each magnifies the other unending
races in time to perfection hurdles over
guiles and subterfuge, your jumps sublime
only for new ones to appear unending

the good towers, disappears in the skies
summons your head, writes lines on your face
words tumble on words each triumphant
discernible to minds coached in knowledge- and- love
announce to the world here lives a soul
travelling through skies to fulfilling joy

19
the nerves came to their senses

you should come and see her now. Did you see her
    then, rooted to the spot
choose any word that says I don' t like you
that would serve these nerves. Thrown out of place
    they seek fresh empires
think they rule the world because they help us think
and we conduct all our connections in highways of
    nerves
the brain disagrees, he's the king and the rest mere
    errand boys
is the servant greater than his master?

the nerves are afraid they get an ultimatum
sprout out and live or
lie here causing pain getting abused not loved
not caressed, all your endings entwined

the nerves came to their senses
we've done our worst let's do our best for the one we
    once loved
madam stand up and walk to the matron walk to the
    nurses
watch them collapse on emerald joy

20
pain in joyful despair

the flavour of pain comes in the ridges of the song
the back, the spine unhinged seeks its bolts all fallen
restructuring needed, must hold the mind to its song

the body conjures up vineyards for untutored tastes
tongues seek salvation produce wines well aged
human joys evaporate sing new songs for heaving
    harvest

tubers of yams planted on ridges shake off pain
through rains and suns and moon and tides
they need nerves to grow in fibres bulging for songs

its flavours disgruntled pain is bitter seeks revenge
the tubers run in ridges embattle pain to its final
    death
and put on a dance in singing flames

21
seventy plus one

on a star studded sky wholesomely ecstatic
seventy stars watch and wait
nature erupts salutes one year added
what shall we say that's not been said, what shall we
    do that's not been done
a new star is born her music the hills proclaim and
    trees prostrate
no one knows what knowledge she brings,
    tomorrow's noon will tell

truth swirls around twisted bones, straightens,
    bends, all is righted
orchestras celebrate the arrival, moons and suns and
    skies and stars
dance their hosannas, knees and joints and bones
    parade their pride
for one taller by one, prophets foretell, the mountains
    rise
numberless pains their fury exhausted, crumble
    unfeeling stones
supreme delight declares a feast for one seventy-one

22
sleep on the valley

down the valley to my home my rest
my peace my love lying low I seek nothing
all is here where heartbeats are scored
flowers of rains cooled in the grass
rainbows curl and end in the field
quiet, solemn my bed in the valley
I roll down the hill into your waiting eyes

23
horses unbroken

little drops from heaven light the sky
drive joys to buckling rodeos
horses unbroken throw off the rider
stars asleep rest the fight friendship awakened

little drops from heaven light the sky
pearls divine, beaded praise, adorn your neck
it's time to sleep. You hair shames the dark
each strand plucks the guitar serenades the sheets

little drops from heaven light the sky
girls rise to mountains, slide down glaciers
men in their pajamas join the party
feet faster than antelopes step to jazz

24
my time

little boy little jacket little shoes
shies away from the sun looks downwards
written on his face innocence
this world is for me for you
let's go and play run around
fetch water from the stream

the sun rises the sun sets, rises again
we say it's a new day, why could it not
be yesterday when the sun returned
to his origin, found joy in the stream
went for some water to quench tomorrow's thirst
not yet announced, he just rolls on and on

why, the warm sky he saw yesterday
today it's all clouds and rain, grey
they tell him yesterday is over
that time moves on to nowhere
he does not understand the cycles
he sees himself growing taller by the day

he goes to sleep wakes up eats his cereals
runs around eats some *moi moi*[1] and orange
runs around eats rice and stew with meat
then sleeps, why do I sleep he asks

---

[1] *Moi moi* is a steamed bean cake.

can't I stay awake watch TV join dad
sit by his side, stroke his face, his mustache?

I wake up to a new day. I wonder, is it new
what is new about this sky, what will it do today
won't it be still the sky, won't the sun still be the sun
they tell me the moon has gone to sleep, will wake
up when the tides swim to shore a thousand times
thousand times, that tides announce the moon
dad tells me: now you don't understand, you're only

a child soon you'll know what it all means
and the world you see now won't be there for you
you're only a child pure and innocent, wile's a
    stranger
do you know when you were born, do you know
when you were in your mom's tummy and she
bore you so sweetly everyone said she'll have
a wonderful baby. That was five years ago

time then sits with me and rides on my back
I must take him wherever I go and make him
my friend, as I was in mama's tummy
he too will live in me and stay with me not
for nine months no, not for a year, it will be
in futures endless, I will be time and time will be me
I shall be as I am now. He will help me for we are
    one
whatever is good about time will ever live in me

25
cover yourself

cover yourself in work don't take it off
till it's soaked on sweat washed in the storm
dried in the sun bruised by love

26
fly in roasted lamb

plantations spread their wings, come to life in his
    presence
the growers serenade the coffee, shake their heads
    full circle
their frenzied necks confound their minds
coffee stems engage themselves in dance
Fella's heavy beats float through acres of green
    delight

the new manager cultivates seedlings jazz their
    manure
swaying with the beat his friendship strokes the
    leaves
the air swiftly completes the symphony all is astir
this manager lives on the soil with the coffee
    growths
all owed to his happy workers, their food his dinner
    too

sitting in the verandah this empty dreary day,
    nothing
to recommend it to joy, the sun far off in deep sleep
coffee for company as black as the skies, no sugar
he drank full the inviting aroma the liquid jealous
for a while only. Lips tongue and cheeks feed their
    desire

plantations still green cry exasperation
when will it be our turn to grace your table fill your
    cup
soon my blossoms soon my berries your burnt life
bespeaks your resurrection, chants your life in my
    cup
your tomorrows in dark splendour race downhill.

coffee thrashing his zeal Agam saunters in Alvaro
    exults
had not seen him since high school days, so much to
    tell
the cup is all ears stories fall over each other, love is
    renewed
wow haven't seen you in years my dear Agam tell me,
    how are you
share this coffee with me from the plantations you
    can see uphill
they saw you and furiously ran down to serve you
    their joys
they've been waiting for a new life in my gardens
lay out the feast, they say, let roasted lamb leap in
    mirthful minds

27
the untold story of all that meets the eye

the introit lights the face with promises over thorns
    and parents' blessings
wrapped in brown paper for Little Boy running to
    offertory with gifts, bringing
incense at communion as DNA helices unravel. Little
    Boy now grown man
a virgin to marry, leaps from woman to wisdom in
    unmasked tutorials
written on drums, tango the beat, his brains
    enraptured in dreams helical enraptured in life's
    dancing coils

28
tracks lined up to walk

Obetiti. A moment a lifetime runs races in tracks over
    my soul
answers find questions and more dreams, planets
    unknown

mysteries unfurl overtake me make me a coward
water runs in my eyes

Obetiti absorbs me the planets rejoice
mysteries dance creation conducting

29
alive in my shadows

my shadows sing me to sleep
morning comes and blinds their eyes

my being takes flight from me
where it goes defines my name

a world of my shadows no trees around
explains me in their stance to forests ungrown

30
little boy

Christ the King School that's where I was taken
by a father pushing for the greatest in
a lad a big rascal truant won't obey any rules
nor keep quiet nor learn his sums
can't add or subtract good for nothing you would say

the teacher's whip sends boy sky bound
turbulence aplenty, his stormy flight
undeterred, whips his aircraft into a frenzy
makes it fly smoothly on bumpy seas
frozen air, lapping waves, no contenders for faith
bring in tarred roads, their stones all raise their

    heads
littleness now supreme must guide the plane as

it flies through nineteen forty-four a year the sun
    shut down
its rays, all captured in his pocket, nighttime arrives
bring out the drums he wants to dance even when

the air's frozen the land swampy all mired in
    nineteen forty-six
but it's not yet nineteen forty-seven the turning point
nineteen forty-eight, supreme delight, swings in
    poetry
the end in sight, sums and words arrange a fiesta for
    one
good for literature, transcending heights his plane
    soars

31
Nwankpi

I can't believe this
at seventy-seven I am the oldest
surviving son of Nwankpi[2] my great grandfather

he was a first class *dibia*[3]
acquired the mythical name Nwankpi after
he changed himself into a butting he-goat
and butted down his opponent another *dibia*
who had challenged him
and my great grandfather won the duel

---

2 A he-goat

3 A traditional medical pracitioner

what does that make me, a dueling firebrand

    that burns all that's untoward?
butts down subterfuge, obsessive
    concupiscence, bears all that's true
thanks to genes my great grandfather gave me I can
    bear butt and burn

32
my memoirs (not yet)

never thought I would write
the story of my life!

that would change after reading
Olugbolahan tell us about his life

I'm the oldest child of Nwankpi
my great grandfather a conquering *dibia*
my task to protect the legend, how he   transformed
to a butting he-goat and crushed his garrulous
    opponent

my cucumber life flat on taste
richly entertains the palate with
tales of Burgundy wines

chameleon's colours paint the lips
yes I shall tell a story the adjectives would love
the adverbs dance joyously the verbs have juju
    nouns

for one their own and pronouns ponder
the transformation from butting he-goat to cell
    biologist

33
seedless you

I had wanted grapes, red
for some time now there were none
settled for white, plummy, natural seeds and all
disappointed, they had only seedless grapes

I told them God must
have known what he was doing
from his garden grew seeded grapes
seeds were part of his creation

seedless, freshness, how do you dance
without seeds the drums are light
no heavy beats that move the heart
care is not needed the trumpet sounds flat

seeds lift my tongue to pursue the hills
seek vineyards of Helenic delight
love animated spreads rich soil
grants a license for seeded grapes

a feast announced, the vineyards agog
pick out their best for that dance supreme
unseeded fruits their hips held high
fall into arms affectionately seeded

34
somewhere

I've been reading Stephen Spender
his poems, wanting to write
some, my own. They form in my head
sit there nowhere to go then vanish
they have a life all their own
somewhere somehow in someone else

35
and I'm not eighty

you would say just three years more
well it's not 'just', it's a mighty time yet in the sky
what will the coming three years say to me
that is, if they come, where are they now

where do you look
time steps out, her violins
no world to play to
not yet a birthday
over each other they lie
await their prompt
the bow steps out
the party can begin

the old man's photo
a double-breasted suit

gives him a regal air not yet his
whatever a suit can do the mind rebuilds

from one second to the next
one smooth faced the other bearded
restive mustache proudly summons distant forests
years rush in, flowers fruit, and eighty
    flamboyants celebrate

36
it's only tennis

you stayed never went away that I may ever have you
the ball is in my court and I don't know the stroke
that matches your infinite love sweeping my heart
the ball bounces, races forth high above my head
can't smash can't bring my volley low, my racket
    gasps
it's all my fault for your spins are there to train me
to run, prepared for any onslaught in whatever form
your ball packed with grace bounces, dragged by sin
    I fall
my arms can't hold me up, my knees buckle my eyes
    darken
knees bloodied, elbows scraped, my tongue in coils
your racquet high, ready for a serve you urge me on:
it's only tennis and you've turned it into arrows and
    pains
just return the ball and watch my winds sail over the
    net

the ball in tow. I'll help you in every way that tennis
is played
your virtues in flower will drive the ball to courts
unseen

37
what's all this

where do you want to spend your time
at home with friends or at the airport alone
solitary you sit glued to a seat
newspaper in hand the plane hours away

it's the unknown I could die going home

38
is it boring

I look at you flow into eternity
your eyes where do they come from
what do they say how do they speak

they draw me into your soul
transcendental bliss enchanting
the heavens dance in your eyes

39
marriage in orbit

feast of dreams bliss undreamt of
our eyes open our tongues in song, the forests
    drum
a new creation without sight or brains, only a   mind
a vast empire, called forth to proclaim and explain

enter Ms mind and examine, tell me what alive
    means
life on skies higher and higher, the utmost at its
    finest
details of a person now defined, eternity races
where are the tools for this uncreated living, where
    its blood
eyes now crystals survey space, planets' orbits
    unknown
created self, self-less, transcends reality
mind in turmoil, without thoughts, a new evolution
in the making, self loses personhood, seeks another

what you encounter may be priceless or your doom
who does the seeking where sight is fragmented
call it love, reasons are not sought, all is ecstasy
it's marriage in orbit, one meddlesome mind found
    another

40
along the way time came upon me

where did I start this journey that seems to take me
    far and out of reach
if I do not know where I started from how would I
    know my beginning
I must have been somewhere dashing from one
    happiness to another
did I collapse and suddenly become someone else or
    something else
and so lost my identity my personality my
    uniqueness by which I'm known
is it really important that I am known, by whom and
    for what purpose
can't I just go on not minding who I am or what I
    might turn out to be

the vastness has come upon me and time pursues
    me to define me
I am lost, only time can find me in this vastness that
    leads nowhere
no, I was not going to any place because I did not set
    out to go anywhere
the earth found me, was proud of me and wanted to
    show off just a little
spun me around, broke off from its orbit and went
    seeking other friends
still bearing me I got too heavy for carriage as its
    axis was now wobbling

I was flung off and soon coalesced with other heavy
    bodies now too heavy
this is all I can remember before I became human
    with a mind a body a soul
can't fly off anymore, can't meet other bodies, I have
    fresh uniqueness

41

you were not on the cards

*'As your children, Uzoma, Onyema, Ikem and myself will
    thank you until eternity*
*for being (in daddy's words) his 'redemption' with your
    grace, elegance,*
gentleness, hospitality, patience and endurance.'

my appointment letter read:
you are appointed Education Officer (Science)
Government Secondary School, Owerri

no, not Owerri, dreamt of a life in a fresh city
there to live my youth in vigour and dalliance
where no one knew me, no one would keep track of
    what I did
or did not, master of my fate I would live in arresting
    vitality
no. Not Owerri. Nothing to offer!

the equation written you were neither in the numbers
    nor the symbols
all speak research, development, the Wenner Gren
    Institute
Stockholm Sweden flying flags of unsurpassed
    quests
my heart breaks into song, John Runstrom on sax
    Olov Lindberg strings

Tryggve Gustafson beats huge African drums rolled
    in from Owerri

buffet laid out the equation goes straight to the wines
fills her glass then mine *Vosne Romanee* warms her
    smiles

Wenner Gren excitedly announces: I have been
    waiting for you
now I can a have a life, study my antecedents
know my beginnings, my destination yet
    unforeseeable
your thesis will expound, that the world may dance
    to musical helices
Tryggve the master will lead you to orchestras of
    mystical embryos

marriage has no place here, not yet time for
    fertilization
the eggs are still resting, not sweeping, no
    fertilization
their life a hymn yet unsung, the words mystical
they sleep they wait for that superb occasion
    singularly divine

no you were not on the cards, keep your eggs in their
    yielding shields
my dream, go for PhD. soar to unreachable heights
undreamt of, prove to the world you have brains not
    made of garri

you showed up. From your Valedictory Lecture:
'Along the way a Volkswagen stopped
and when I looked inside one of the two
occupants was the very education officer
I had been introduced to....
and by the time he brought us back from Mass
I had made up my mind
I knew I would marry this man.'

you were not on the cards. How could this be?
where did you come from?
you leave me breathless, dreams climbing on hills
where owls dare the sun, fly and frolic at mid-day
speak to minds rising to distant hills their tops
    dizzying
soaked in sordid ventures unfit for mention, body
    scarred
years of dirt dragging bags bedraggled, all is decay
cockroaches rats geckoes long dead on beds bruised
infect my soul, repentance not in sight what will save
    me
I have no remorse it's all rotten tomatoes in a feast of
    dissonance
you showed up, clothed rainbow, beauty
    overwhelming
I saw you. My world ran from your head to your toe
    to your eyes

I was lost, unforeseeable dreams undreamt capture
   me
transport me to heavens not yet built, awaiting my
   mettle

to give life a world mellifluous. Helen, my dream, my
   redemption
in heaven before God you sing and dance and plead
save my husband Mark, wash him clean of dirt
his lights unseen, make him dazzle me

a poem on Helen Anurukem meeting Mark Nwaguru in Owerri in 1961 before their marriage soon after. The Wenner Gren Institute, Stockholm, Sweden, where Mark did his PhD., had Prof. John Runnstrom as the first director of the institute and Prof. Olov Lindberg as the current director, when Mark was there, 1962-1965. Prof. Tryggve Gustafson was Mark's research supervisor (MN).

42
being

how is it dark everywhere
when the sun in its splendour shines its purest rays
if we are deaf are we blind or, perhaps, we've turned
our back on all that's good, neither beauty nor song
cheers our heart, we shine our own lights
sing dirges, doing whatever pleases our mangled
    minds

our crops, a new life they embrace, and flourish
    before
our very eyes, assure us nature is agog and brilliant
and we do not see we do not hear, our feelings have
raced off to the Himalayas, frozen in the cold our
    noses brittle
crack and waste away even as we struggle to patch
    up
our broken brains, no use for dreaming
what has happened to us that we're thus, the sun
    ashamed
all that's good forsakes us, flees from our
    bedraggled bones
wake up my people, the spirits stir, we've got a long
    way
to meet our fervid souls.

born in grace our souls awaken burnished
bright lights weave baskets of our being

43
I'll put you in my pocket

I'll put you in my pocket take you wherever I go
whether it's my new suit, my school clothes
my pyjamas, there you'll be quietly resting
to be put to use when I call, lay my head
on you to gather my thoughts into place
plant them in your seeds to grow new roots
new energies tall in the sun mature to knowledge
you will teach me and I'll grow with you
branch out reach the ends of the earth
I pull out the last mystery, dance in your smiles

44

rains for Waithira

mind slips away for a dance in the field heavy rain
 pouring
each drop a thought wets the hair, the scalp revels,
 conjures
mustached masquerade wearing bamboo leaves,
 bamboo stems its feet
mind races on finds Waithira soaked in the rain
what could this be?
may I have a have a dance with you my dear

yes you may I've not danced since I collapsed into
 Kili-man
they swing into the lightning, thunder keeps the beat
bamboo legs shuffle, ease into movement
command minds to flee
spins damsel a thousand times, Kilimanjaro erupts
Thira resurrects, tangled, they tango to thunders

*I pay my respects to 'Scent of A Woman', a movie with
Al Pacino that taught me that you can tango tangled.
(MN)*

45
word for words

what is it you would like me to say about you

then I ask myself what do I know about you
and suddenly waves and waves of thoughts
rise higher and higher on the still seas of my mind

what do I do when the seas speak words above my
    head
goad me to understand impressions of ruined justice
you write judgments favourable for both plaintiff and
    accused

whichever you read sings songs of surfing scandal
this is what I know ladies and gentlemen of this man
    before you

my thoughts float atop the clouds, conscience
    weightless
mind leaves the body airless, space seeks me out,
    holds my hands

he is a scoundrel, minted monies his bedside
    romance

46
closeness aroused

despoiling discharges threw him to the sidewalk
    closeness forbidden
his clothes, the holes the size of his skull scampered
    over his cloak
the crust of a fortnight's foraging blessed his bleeding
    gums
the hair gripped tightly to the head each strand a
    million dollars
grown out of a Goldman Chase career hunting heads
all is now washed into the sewers, nothing more to
    sell or destroy
homeless disheveled despoiled, all is stench
friendship a cousin from Mars too far off for humans

must love Bobo as he is—externals discarded in
    praise of dirt
bring down Mars he must, enclose Bobo in friendship
    embrace his details
took him home, scrubbed him, the wastes rushed
    forth darkly escaping
teeth mouth tongue gushed slime, words glued to the
    palate
five buckets of water, two brushes with freshly
    minted toothpaste
new pants t-shirt long sleeved shirt, and a gentleman
    emerges

thanks and gratitude tumble, nouns butt verbs head
    to head
the dictionary perplexed creates new words only for
    Bobo.

his features ruthlessly restored, a good night's sleep
summons repentance, his spirit brilliant, glistening
conduces friendship, closeness, an ally, sits on his
    smiling eyes
dreams chase his vision to heights unspoken,
    success whispers (again)

47
Alex Ekwueme

You've seen people dealt with people
faith in minds, with wings spread out
betrayal strides in all virtues in flight
the rainbow forsaken, colours ashen

guns start booming, birds flee from tree to tree
bullets seeking feathered prize
pierce one for dinner another for sale
let them flee who can

he rose to escape weighed down
bones heavy head of hair a forest
feet planted on the ground
can't run can't grow wings

guns start booming at legs on ground
armoured in faith he stands in defiance
people arrive sing thousand hosannas
the eagles return fly all to virtue

they twirl around Alex in a feast of fortitude
hopping to nectar of *Flame of the Forest*
all is joy the birds announce
heavens exult draw us to homing heights

48
Kpakpando

my name is *Kpakpando*[4] my land fertile will bear fruit
start low crawl if you may, whistle even shout
your presence announced the oracles awake
a new dawn rises perspicacity pregnant

where's the beginning where the script where the
    rondo
trunks herald the climb, girded champions seek new
    heights
it's all evergreen, leaves and tendrils and spines
    conspire
stalwarts dethroned their climb thwarted fall to their
    knees

my name is *Kpakpando* my land fertile draws down
    new stars
lights incandescent, trumpets blast, seduce virgin
    blossoms
the orchestra untrammeled, strings astir, rondo in
    crescendo
the rainbow unfurls, green grasps yellow, red
    embraces violet

---

4 Star

I am *Kpakpando* the earth my theatre Ibadan her
   home
orange invites indigo in dance, my mind their
   costume
the feast is set, angels lead me blindfold, announce a
   world
Kpakpando Brightest Star of all, you are seventy

happy birthday, 'Femi Osofisan

49
the Cambridge sisters

Baraah, Cheryl and Funeke, the Cambridge Sisters,
   they called themselves
before they had a name for the group, changed their
   lodgings
after living in Canada, shared a three-bedroom flat,
   each with its bathroom

theirs was a large kitchen and, as their daily lives
   varied from person to person, each cooked her
   meals separately. Lunch was available at college
   and they had their dinners depending taste &
   trimmings

Baraah found the cafeterias did not have her kinds of
   vegetarian foods and gave up lunching totally,
   waited until she came home and could prepare

something for herself. Cheryl, on the other hand,
very much used to English cuisine had

her lunch and dinners at college. Funeke just could
not find her usual Xhosa foods anywhere and
adapting to English foods was an uphill task.
Baraah would cook meals for everyone her veggie
discipline much extant. Would meals separate us?

no I'll cook for all of us, all you want, all you can eat,
that we may remain one

50
Ibadan to and fro

just back from Ibadan where....
Ibadan is not just a place, heaven is not just a place
heaven runs through your soul flows in your veins
erupts in your eyes for you to see the universe

heaven escapes mere earthly words
you need heaven's world to speak the language there
so what is Ibadan that defies of-this-earth dictionary
oh! it's this crystal university floating on Awba dam

51
where's that

there's a place where we can learn new laughters
    where our legs
will move away from us and play a tune on the big
    drum
hoisted on top of palm trees all of them tall and only
    the sky can dance

this is not our place, no it's not our place, where it is,
    what it's like
we don't know, can't feel which is air and which wind

there's a place where our past would be dinner
    served every morning
coffee black, white wine, Chardonnay, whistle our
    thoughts loud

all life's journeys consumed in seven or so servings
    each with a new chef
little drops of the moment rise on the wineglass seek
    a home
the top enamored serenades the future builds her a
    castle

52
shine forth brightly (again)

meetings build foundations, humble skyscrapers
not rightness not wrongness, let it rain
soothing waters wash tables of searing words
meaning reigns in flaming truth

53
sleep more sleep
sleep more sleep it does not change, can't be
    anything else
sleep more sleep starts the fight, my will unyielding
    wants to
sleep, more sleep all is wasted where there's no
    sweaty work
sleep more sleep, time in sympathy girds his loins
    holds him
leads him to the garden to commence work, weeding
    proceeds
the guest does not notice his host, his mind in
    disarray
time rushes in screams aloud, all can hear except
    sleep's guest
blind he reaches out for the pillar but it's sand
    nothing to hold to
hairs raised, he tries to regain self, 'was I not alive a
    while ago'

jumps into the pool swims eight lengths muscles
    exhausted
he slumps, time rushes in brings in sleep, more sleep

54
today is not just any day

the queen who gives us a king
bears us to him before he's born
he made her, how can this be,
the mother gives us a beginning
before there's a beginning, how can she
be there before there was 'there'
has a a face before she was created
to mother a king

plain circle called a square is still
a circle, a circle it remains
what will be already exists
our today's roads to yesterday that never was

she's queen, she's mother, she kept
it all in her heart that our futures
a mystery, my live today
today, and today

55
death for the beast

evening comes spreads its wings unfolds the beast
morning sun announces its rage summons brave
    hearts
gallant knights ere nightfall go to battle
the beast in flight offers all, a feast of deaths

I'll die for them and they'll be saved
the beast is beaten her wings in flames
a new life begins the people exult
virtues eternal sing hosannas

56
forty plus nine

those alive only count
the day they have, today
what of all the yesterdays
each with tendrils searching

where to embrace
to kiss
the tips touch maybe retract
back to self

out they stretch one more time

fresh welcomes to find
that today may curl around all other days
in warm embrace and fulsome smile

rainbow colours wear a testament
announce the years sewn in harmattan haze
and august rains
a harvest forty-nine

happy birthday Uzoma

57
David waves welcome

a low carbon event, emission. Don't contaminate
hydrogen finds oxygen they dance, breathing life
flow around heads, necks stretch, the skies eagerly
    wait
drink up the water no clouds are formed and all is
    again dry

oxygen races seeks hydrogen's hand a new dance in
    swing
drums beat their joy, clouds form
oxygen hydrogen father and mother await the child
rivers swallow new waters, humans are soaked,
    sands glisten

the skies, hands outstretched welcome all airs clean
    unclean

create a basket, sieve out dirt that the good may flow
oxygen hydrogen lift their son to Himalaya
David on Everest waves all welcome.

58
welcome to Freedom Garden

cabbage carrots peas await to be served
have not seen this table for a long time
the peas in revolt fan away conspiring sands
friendly carrots gave them passage

the sands escape to their home soils
and gather manure
for growths of peas
wholesome greens, palates their destiny

59
childhood

the autonomous republic
of make believe...

childhood

inspires visions of
unsuspected palaces

60
spaces primed for walls

prime time I am told
it must be done now or
else failure will wrap us
and tie us to the wall

failure your face all smiles
is failure death
you jump down then fall
is this failure

walls, we need spaces
free, empty, filled with air
that we may breathe
free to fly airborne

61
the appointment

could not remember if we would meet in my office or
        hers
was running late on the wheels Helen called her
she would not mind coming to my office
two big bags one on each shoulder accompanied her

first bag whistles childhood ages five to twelve
recalls breakfast eggs scrambled yoghurt excites
morals and virtues toast their welcome laughter
        lounges
morning dew drapes the wineglass hastens recall

second bag brings a lifetime, *Vosne Romane* regales
full bodied red, wheels in adventures through
    adulthood
a drink to fortitude another to chastity crystal pure
'versity life celebrates freedom choices untoward beg
    to leave

the bones ready for a dance shout their joy beat the
    drums
success brings *Hennessy*, dessert aglow schooling
    conquered
now a surgeon she cuts through flesh offences
    repaired
nature's vineyards serve smiling burgundies Dozie
    sparkles

62
Obetiti dreams

a moment a time a day a year a lifetime all whisper
Obetiti
search meaning, in thoughts in dreams in sorrows
Obetiti
running races in tracks over tracks of my soul
    colliding
Obetiti
answers provided dreams ascending
Obetiti

63

she runs

mysteries confound me
I fall off the cliff
roll into her
she stands holding me
in creation running

Happy Valentine 2018 Helen
may we run to forever

64
where are you

the lines are straight
form squares where they will
determined they run along
form larger squares. A prism

circumscribed, silence reigns
all seems resolute. Refined

precise you would say, regular
becomes energized space

nowhere to go and nothing to form
only squares. Throw in some circles
and the dance is on, round and round
we go, until we tip over

at the edge of a square
spaces unknown welcome us

to the mermaids' dance
waltz and tango in ocean circles

65
body triumphant

oh it's so cold this morning I want to run to heaven
hang on to God himself his warmth infinite
meters can't measure the rise and fall
of my heaving despair, coagulating

what can live finds a place pleasing
the soul cools or heats itself peace the therm
if there's a self with separate needs, body triumphant
withdraws into soul, temperature rising icebergs
    thaw anon

66
freedom fighter

weighed down buffeted by all around me
soul at rest no pains anywhere just unglued
can't make sense of a world that knows only self
self pleases self, self seeks self, self stands on self
however I look at it, it ends up a circle without exit
that's not my life, my self is made for the other

within tribes the other is the enemy, he warns
and I answer, it's all lost in diatribe

67
faith you have a flip side

oh I have faith it's quite strong too!
it comes and goes and leaves me to myself
I forget and it wanders off doesn't come back
my humanness in charge of all I do
has nature not given me these attributes to deal with
    life
as best I see fit, using my natural intellect
all goes well but not quite, tiredness creeps in
strangles my legs, holds them down
cements me to the floor my brains bruised
memory does not legs move, nor hands shake
the floor a friend keeps me from falling
where else could I fall, there's the end

where is my faith?

68
shirt & tie

sitting there in shirt and tie, shirt grey, blood-red
    burgundy tie
five years of toil, each day written on a hair grey and
    glistening
the smile sums up seven score years and more spent
in the lab, varieties of eggs waiting to hatch or not
    hatch
to be chickens chirping on the grass or eggs their
    whites
boiled and the yellows scrambled in wait for
    breakfast

69
in helical joys

a moment a time a day a year a lifetime all whisper to
    Obeititi
search meaning in the mind, in thoughts in dreams
    in sorrows
running races in tracks over tracks of my soul
    colliding, disappearing
more dreams float in planets unknown, Obetiti
    dismayed
conquering mysteries overcome me, freeze up my
    eyes
self is lost, absorbed into Helen, Jewel of Obetiti
    warms my face

and I can see her, the planets rejoice, her eyes their
    axis
she spins from head to toe holds me entwined in
    helical joys

Happy Valentine 2010, Helen

70
Obetiti

Obetiti your summons, words unspoken
unwritten, buried, the mines of your soul their home
I search for meaning where all I have is space
you lift me turn me around and drop me in wonder

Obetiti depths unreachable pull me down
darkness lit by blinding gems unsearchable
joy immeasurable, my eyes unspeakable heavens
immortality shines forth proclaims my ancestors

Obetiti here I am your doorstep beckons, your
    garments
adorn me, make me ready for the wedding feast
your ancestors awake to hosannas rising by the hills
where saints dance, their joy joined to the rainbow

Obetiti mother of mothers your womb a lab supreme
theories extreme seek answers beyond
    understanding
rumble endlessly, the best joins heads with laggards
unschooled, the answers known only to Stony River

your womb the world itself: trees nestle with giraffes
twirling tendrils seek support, irokos stalwart chant
     their welcome
palm trees celebrate, wave their 'kerchiefs conjure a
     vision
one of their own, like no other, bears signs supremely
     configured

Obetiti dreams return, eager to burst out of mindless
     spaces
mines conquered, diadems long since buried, find a
     new face
nature resplendent, virtue her necklace, finds fellows
     genteel
birth prism dazzles, drumming babies dance *abigbo* [5]

71
silent rhythms

Chioma tradition never dies
what makes me Okeosisi will live on in you
what I saw you will see with different eyes
all things have their place in time and continuity
nothing good ever dies
any good I have been able to do with my life
will live on in you. And you will pass it on.

---

5 A traditional dance of Mbaise, where Obetiti
is located.

72
tempests unsung

eagle-flying skies
bear scoundrels
on winging eyes

gems unknown
erupt from seas
build pyramids prismatic

73
it was once here

you ruined the view, it's lost to me
and what do I have, it's only you standing there
the sky curls in escape of your lightning and
    thunder
that soon burst into fire consuming the air we
    breathe

now you've left, the view arrests your coat tails
her cave your dwelling place selfishly consuming
we climb the escarpment search your frontiers
how do I describe what I can't see or see only if
    asleep

and when do I sleep when all I do is stand here
waiting for the view my grandfather said was his
    village
I fall asleep ah! my eyes awake to a new existence
a little hut, bamboo thatched roof and mud-wall
    lizards

I run to the roof higher and higher it grows
to the very ends of the sun. The universe exults
Obetiti's perfumes aflame, I'm consumed in extant
    skies
my village my world cascades in grandfather
    enshrined

74
to feel not to know

if you want to see spirits look at surrealist paintings
whether of your own making or in the mind of the
    painter

you will spin and turn as you follow the strokes
questions you will ask you'll not find answers
the spirits cannot help you
they only want your mind to live the paintings

75
Avilla your air is Theresa

she lived here centuries ago I 'd like to see her home
I don't know where it is, will call where I am her
    home
all parts of this town shout Theresa
I'll find where you pour out your breath, feed on it,
    wear your spirits

I want to find your place Theresa touch the walls
where you lived your home clothed in warmth and
    love
no it's not the walls I seek, your heart Theresa your
    heart

pour your love into me lift me to the heavens give me
    a new name
I could be created again where I am in this garden
take a picture with you to show here I met Theresa of
    Avilla
forever it will hold memories of your beating heart
your blood flowing through me makes me do as you
    did

to catch the sun skies warm, don't leave me
I live on the air you breathe flowing all over me

76
where is nine

I am here because you want us to be here
others, nine of them, danced to the river, douched
    their disease
there is something I can give, my heart my poor heart

with little blood, squeeze and squeeze only drops drip
    out
or my love, see how fast I walked
even dancing to your music when I got closer

you moved me to go on and I went on
yes it was no longer tedious
I offer all of me in every stride I take
my hips swiveling to your call unstoppable

77
distance

I'm so sleepy
there seems to be an infinite
distance between
where I was for a week
and where I am now
Lagos
I can't live in Madrid
it is Lagos
and that makes me sleepy
hoping I wake up in Madrid

78
please don't go

it is time to go to sleep, it is dark. The sun
guardian of light brilliant shines all over my
    world
tells me he will now go and show himself to
    Japan
I tell him I can't sleep, there are tanks
    everywhere

79
chest out

straight up chest out Don has the answer
mind twirls, new tendrils seek out encounters
encircle the fathers, coil round them, pull their roots
resurrection is announced, father and son rise in joy

80
confidence an engineer

engine cylinders fire up down up down
motion transferred to other motions
one vertical the other horizontal, and wheels run

looking down he thinks
what do I need now, how do I
find an answer to this problem
no fuel for my engines. The journey beckons

realities thin out return as prayers
travel east wake up the sun
darkness peels away reveals fleeing truths
the earth turns west the sun grants his last rays

furious engines turn turbines of his heart
new eyes lensed see promises galloping
armies of answers flood his face, his orange eyes
race eastwards win fuel for tomorrow's wheels

81
the universe dances

the universe dances, the earth spreads her wings
bears each child on a leaf, eternity her roots

her eyes light the skies announce a baby born
time races, crowns her queen, heaven and earth
   rejoice

82
you come looking

you come looking nobody told me
what it is you want you gave me no notice
so you'll get whatever you can find
this place is mad the floor muddy

I need to be ready for all sorts of strangers
this is my place the pillars reflect my soul
nothing solid to hold my head keep it upright
my eyes can't see they've run into holes in the mud

can't come down to earth where rivers and seas
seize the land, all is salty sand, can't yield a harvest
where would I grow my oranges my guavas even
    mangoes

don't come looking for fruits till I have fertile land
perhaps I'll rot, turn to manure feed the orchard
yield some avocados, my blood in their skin

83
strength lies in confusion

my last steps grow weak sleep straddles my eyes
curves my spine draws knees rheumatic to my lips
can't help myself, must stand tall close the day firmly
you whisper: strength lies in confusion

stripes, black breaks into white, here narrow
there wide, thins out at the top
your enemies are confused bewildered exasperated
your eyes drink up energy, open, your walk brisk
you can now return to your tasks
and it is goodnight

84
freedom at last

they wail, the world flying off the sky hanging low
angels are grounded the heavens despoiled
earth and sky shake hands, tears wash their faces
you see them their loads on their backs heavy
they run east they run west they seek utopia
there's no escape all frontiers are surrounded
exits must be found or bloodshed the outcome

a man red with blood, hair burnt red eyes dropping
the face bland, stretched into lonely despair
his right foot a size seven in size ten shoes black
left foot wrapped with straws wound tightly
he lost his world lifetimes ago
nothing much to claim in today's lovelessness
oversize head, beard gray, sweeping the grass
eyes bloodshot from bullets that cut off his nose
his hands off their sockets blistered and battered
the air above his head buries his smiles beneath his
     feet

a young couple strapped together float above
    weaponed
they fall into his laps and laughter finds his sliced
    cheeks

we found a way in you, tomorrow we'll row to Obetiti

85
butterfly nine

I count you off each a butterfly wearing all shades of
    red
by the time I get to nine it's like blood itself
but you don't know this, you've never seen blood
today will be different, each in fluttering red seeks

    stigmas
of nectarine blood, a new meal all configured to feed
    nourished hearts
but you don't have hearts nor feelings, you just fly

    not knowing where

unlike all others you know you have real blood
you have a heart readied to fly, I count the rest off
the ninth wearied, its crimson wings flapping and

    flapping collapse and fall
I watch, step in, get close, lift her up, we climb a tree
almost at the top I bear you on the back of my hand

no need to fly I'll take you there

no I'll get to the top myself, by myself, for the torture
   is only for me
no second heart needed only mine is sought only
   mine will die, he says
what will I do Butterfly Nine at the top with you dying
   I'll stay and watch, tell your story on resurrection
   day

86
daddy just sign

we live our lives in circling orbits each a planet unto
   itself
oblivious of the other consumed in self
only the sun knows our existence, casts light on our
   thoughts
and we begin to discover our true destiny

the marriage explosive one mind erupts engulfed in
   the other
in one ecstatic collision a new planet ensues, another
   orbit created
and love infinite breathes new life in bloods flowing in
   one heart

separation knocks, its sound dizzying, yet compelling,
   planets in fury
death roars in Kojo's brain, issues a warning, kidney
   despoiling

dark ghoulish blood seeks crimson lifeline for beating
     hearts

Kojo's brothers' organs match, his life in ascendance
you must live, they say, we love you both, your
     marriage our pillar
inseparable in life you've got to continue, your
     planet prism unto our hopes

Kojo's father heartless won't let his sons give kidney
     to their brother
warns them, do so and you're banned from my
     presence for life

bemused betrayed bewildered she collapses, all is lost
     what's next
my world still in orbit I must give my kidney to my
     dying husband

we are one, coiling our spirals around each other our
     kidneys match
my kidney would be his and he'd be fine our planets
     circling, still same orbit

daddy please sign the authorization, let me give my
     kidney to Kojo
and I'll again possess my skies, my life, my love

87
he came for us

it was pitch dark everywhere
white snow sunlight of the night
they came for us

my cows bleat louder and louder
more join, it became a nightmare
they came for us

couldn't make it out
sleep strapped me to the bed
they came for us

broke loose, this cannot be
what's going on
they came for us

banging on the door
windows smashed I saw a face
he came for us

roused up my wife
quick quick escape to the attic
he came for us

what did I do wrong
where did I go wrong
he came for me

my head in a quarry
brain turns to stone
he came for me

Lord what are my defences
where my weapons
he came for me

pulled me under the bed
down to the basement
he came for me

pushed me through a break in the wall
escape escape he shouted
he came for me

where are you
here I am free
buried deep in the snow
I've come for you
I looked into infinity
where is my wife
where's Sarah
they came for her

searched the house
frantic furious, attic-bound
they claimed
they came for her

one step two steps
five steps
sixth step up straight

broken, gives way
he came for her

great the fall
no way up
must use a rope

Sarah in tumult
up through the roof
leaped far out

he came for her
led her to me

the killing had started
white blood red snow
he saved us

sixty years on
Sarah and I
children grandchildren
great grandchildren

he lives in us

88
sounds

the storm gathers steam fury his name
thunder gives him a punch
shouts his disaffection
their sounds pronounced rains pour down

89
buried & lost we were once stars

heavy, too heavy stars burn out their lives in
    smashing collisions
self disappears can't be reborn, their ash sings aloud
choruses for fresh marriages governed by touch
new life breathes, self masters self, traditions
    shattered
they leave their ancestral heights nosedive through

    space
the earth their home on a journey from forever to
    today
their meaning harnessed by minds in pursuit of
    dazzling stars
ofe Owerre[6] on fire sizzles, supernovas trillion years
    away rush to the pot

---

6. *Ofe Owerre,* a traditional meal of Owerri: the vegetable soup that
gives Owerri its romantic and irresistible flavour

all the elements arrive, announce their specialties,
    salt pepper oil even crayfish
it's a fable commenced at Eden in the minds of the
    gods who formed it all
that each element may bind to another and another
    in colliding creation

90
till Ikoyi comes to Obetiti

thought you were nothing, mere blocks and pillars
    and open spaces
spread out without arms, only legs and heads.
    everywhere eyes
three floors high you stood, the sky far off not part of
    your dream
you lack ambition, mere three floors when across the
    river
there's Manhattan tall enough to swallow you, turn
    you into toilets
cranes stand over your head supplying parts to make
    you grow
human hands give you a voice, you begin to assume
    life, look alive
craftsmen, their enthusiasm their skills their finesse
    transform you
slowly unnoticeable, your wings your hands spread
    out reach
east and west like a track field ready for Usain Bolt to
    stretch his legs

they gave you life where you were once open ground
    for foxes and squirrels
developers pour in, look around, Manhattan
    beckoning, the pull irresistible
must make a fortune out of the miserable clout of
    hungry charlatans
you were born for the rich, seeking closeness to the
    city their breath speedless
up you rise from depths unfathomable that you may
    tower above them all
tallest and noblest of your generation, these cranes
    must give way to majesty
rising without stop to kiss the skies as they part ways
    for your giraffed neck
the men a class unto themselves labour to shroud

    cement with majesty
elegance seeks comfort among screws and nuts and
    nails driving into walls
staccato structures put up a fight, throw beauty to
    the wind. Give me strength
beauty for the immature reed that bends in the wind,
    knows not where to go
this way that way the breeze fully in command. Not
    me, you say, I will be firm.
I'll be standing here till there's a man on Mars, till
    Ikoyi runs down to Obetiti
rig up water sprinklers, farm on clay soil, produce
    udara[7]

---

7 A delectable juicy fruit indigenous to southern Nigeria

91
it's all sevens

seventy four, thirty seven twice over
my favourite year, in love magnified

all that's good doubling to the Himalayas
the valleys bring in pillows for restful hope

a lifetime together the rice still cooking
growth unending the lilies yet to flower

what's unsurpassed, Helen sublime
God's creation, he took time to make her

Happy birthday Helen

92
timeless rainbows

where did my time go, can't find it
how did I spend my time, the day was full
it jumps and dances unmindful of my cares
your eyes capture time, seize eternity
and I frolic in boundless rainbows

93

If I didn't want to ride *gwongworo*[8] I would not marry you

sincerity traverses the mines

seeks truth, buried
buried deep
waves a fan in elation
gems of truth announce their name
out rushes faith wearing a tie
tip points deeply
pierces unreachable depths
reveals hope a bride bedecked
births families bound by love
that's all that's needed
if I didn't want to ride *gwongworo* I would not   marry
     you
jeweled dynasty grows in honour

---

     public transport, body disheveled, lowest fare

Printed in the United States
By Bookmasters